Marjorie Furlong
Virginia Pill

photography
Marjorie Furlong

WILD
EDIBLE
FRUITS
&
BERRIES

Naturegraph Publishers

Library of Congress Cataloging in Publication Data CIP

Furlong, Marjorie, 1917—
    Wild edible fruits and berries.

    1. Plants, Edible—Northwest, Pacific—Identification.
    2. Food, Wild—Northwest, Pacific. 3. Cookery (Wild foods)
    4. Fruit—Northwest, Pacific. 5. Berries—Northwest, Pacific.
    I. Pill, Virginia B., 1922— joint author. II. Title.

QK98.5.U6F87   582'.06'32   74-32015

ISBN 0-87961-032-8 Paper Edition

Naturegraph Publishers, Inc., Happy Camp, CA 96039

C O N T E N T S

INTRODUCTION

The hunt for the elusive wild berry includes discovering not only the ones plainly visible but also those concealed under old dead limbs and last year's leaves or beneath the stalks of the fearsome nettles, and even those hiding coyly under their own foliage. You and the garter snakes may take turns startling each other—but those cold-blooded, harmless creatures are needed to control the insect population, which appears to be ruining so much of the foliage in our area. A more serious deterrent to berry picking is the weather, as most berries ripen during the hottest days of the year. For blackberry picking it is almost mandatory to wear long sleeves and slacks that afford good protection from the mosquitoes and the prickly, ensnaring vines, though such heavy clothes can get uncomfortably hot.

However, that first bite of a wild blackberry pie will quickly convince the skeptic that it was worth all the inconveniences he may have suffered and the effort expended. Berry picking can be a rewarding family outing, for young and old alike will benefit from the fresh air and exercise involved in the picking, and from the vitamins and minerals obtained in eating the fruit. Berries are valuable for their high content of Vitamin C and for the natural sugars which they contain. Dr. Cleaves, of England, who holds the title of Surgeon Captain, says that our bodies need only the sweetener of a little honey and the fresh berries and fruits we eat. He and many other authorities now believe that many of our degenerative diseases are the result of excessive sugar consumption. You can replace sweet desserts with some of our 42 edible wild fruits and berries for better health. Some of the fruits described also contain protein, other carbohydrates, and fats.

All the berries and wild fruits illustrated and described in this book were found in easily accessible areas, usually not more than a few yards from the road. Most of the fruit was even going to waste! Despite civilization with its pollution and destruction of our wilderness, it is incredibly true that nature has provided an abundance of edible wild fruits and berries.

Since almost all the wild fruits photographed were growing along or near roads, we deplore the spraying or needless cutting of these plants by road maintenance crews, or anyone else. Any plant that produces an edible food and is not a safety hazard should be preserved, not destroyed. We ask you, the forager, to be careful not to harm the plant which produces the fruit or berry, or the surrounding vegetation. There are many places to look for berries: along back-country public roads, in state and national forests, in state and national parks, perhaps even in your own pasture or back yard. Just do not trespass on private lands, and always check with park rangers or others in authority for rules on picking fruits and berries on public lands.

Plant names are based on current authorities. We hope the descriptions and photographs will help the reader identify the more interesting of the many wild fruits. Scientific names as well as some common names for the fruits or berries are given, and a glossary is provided to explain the few unavoidable botanical terms. We urge the reader to be positive of the identification and edibility of a wild fruit before eating it. Take this book with you to the woods so you may compare the photo and text with the plant you have discovered. It is best not to overeat of any new fruit until you know that it agrees with you.

We do not advocate taking large quantities of fruit, especially of those species that are scarce, and especially the ones which mean survival for many birds and other animals; however, it could be valuable to know which are edible if ever needed for survival.

The recipes are included with the hope that they will help the forager realize greater enjoyment from eating the wild fruits and berries.

Twisted Stalk, Liverberry, Scoot Berry
Streptopus amplexifolius   **Lily Family**

Too many of these berries consumed raw have been known to have a cathartic effect on some people—which explains the last common name.

Large ovate leaves grow alternately from the stem. One characteristic of the lily family is parallel veining in the leaves. In May or June, single white or cream-colored, bell-shaped flowers hang hidden under the leaves, along a twisted stem. By late summer, bright red, oblong berries replace these blossoms.

Twisted Stalk prefers shady, damp woods at middle elevations. Found in Washington and across the U.S. in similar areas.

The leaves of the young shoots can be used raw in a green salad. The fruit can be eaten raw in small quantities or made into jelly, using the recipe for Fairy Bells (p. 53).

Twisted Stalk *(Streptopus amplexifolius)*
Picture taken near Lake Cushman, Washington.

7

False Solomon's Seal
Smilacina amplexicaulis   **Lily Family**

Solomon's Seal plants received their name from the power of the fresh or dried roots to heal or seal a wound. From a single stem, the leaves grow alternately, and literally wrap themselves around the stem. These leaves are wider and more heavily veined than those of Star-flowered Solomon's Seal. The creamy star-like flowers blossom in a thick cluster at the end of the stem, in the months of May and June. The unripe fruit is a mottled red and green, but deep red when ripe in late summer. Most berries contain one large pearl-like seed.

Found in moist woods throughout British Columbia and Washington.

The berries may be consumed raw, or made into a jelly (p. 53). Because of the bland flavor, they are best combined with a more acid berry such as Red Huckleberry.

False Solomon's Seal *(Smilacina amplexicaulis)*
Picture taken near Hoodsport, Washington.

Star-flowered Solomon's Seal, Starry Solomonplume
Smilacina stellata   Lily Family

Similar to False Solomon's Seal, this plant comprises a single stem, 1 to 2 feet high, from which long, thin leaves grow alternately. The base of each leaf seems to wrap itself around the stem. From April to June, tiny, star-like, white flowers, 3 to 15 in number, grow in a flame or plume shape from the end of the stem. These are later replaced by green berries with red stripes. Each berry contains about 8 seeds. The fruit takes a long time to ripen, so have patience. The ripe, all-red berries should be ready for picking by late August or early September.

Look for these plants in moist woods throughout Washington from sea level to 3000 feet elevation. You may find them in British Columbia at higher elevations.

You will probably consider them too seedy for jam or pie, but they could be used for syrup (p. 58) or jelly, using the Fairy Bell recipe (p. 53). These berries may be consumed raw, so could be considered survival food or a handy snack for the hiker.

Star-flowered Solomon's Seal *(Smilacina stellata)*
Picture taken near Lake Cushman, Washington.

Fairy Bells

Disporum Smithii and *D. oreganum*   **Lily Family**

Two or three white bells hang on the end of each 1- to 3-foot stem. Shiny, heavily veined leaves successfully hide these flowers, which bloom in May and June. When the orange fruit is ripe, in late summer, the leaves turn a very yellow-green color.

Fairy Bells is found in moist forest areas throughout Washington, Oregon, and northern California.

The fruit is edible raw but is very seedy. Our jelly (p. 53) has a most unusual flavor, not unlike a tropical fruit. Don't miss the opportunity to try it if you find enough berries to make jelly.

Fairy Bells *(Disporum Smithii)*
Picture taken near Hoodsport, Washington.

Oregon Grape, Tall Mahonia, Holly Grape, Creeping Mahonia
Mahonia spp.   Barberry Family

These shrubs vary from about 1 foot tall to as much as 8 feet tall. All species have evergreen, holly-like leaflets which grow on yellow woody stems. The tender, new leaves of Oregon's State Flower are delicious when eaten raw and are considered beneficial for the complexion according to some authors. Bright yellow flowerlets brighten the hillsides in May.

The fruit comprises brilliant blue clusters of roundish berries that are ripe from August to October.

Common from British Columbia to southern California, and from sea level to dry mountain slopes.

The fruit is good for nibbling raw, and delicious made into jam, jelly or juice. The Indians ate the berries raw, cooked them into soup, or used them to flavor their meat, but never dried them. Oregon-grape/apple-juice recipe on page 50.

Tall Mahonia *(Mahonia aquifolium)*   Oregon Grape *(Mahonia nervosa)*

The picture of high-bush was taken at Quilcene, and of low-bush at Lake Cushman, Washington.

11

Gooseberry, Common Wild Gooseberry
Ribes divaricatum   Saxifrage Family

This species of Gooseberry is armed with a spine at each joint of stems that may reach 4 to 6 feet before bending over. The deciduous, three- to five-lobed leaves are arranged alternately along the stems. Their light green color is usually tinged a rusty red by the time the berries ripen.

During April and May look for the purplish or greenish, tiny blossoms with five petal-like lobes, that hang in clusters of one to four flowers. The ripe, smooth, wine-black berries, along with some green ones, are ready to pick by July on into August.

Wild Gooseberries are found in coastal forests and along roadways, from western British Columbia to central California. Other species can be found in swamps and mountains, coast to coast, from Canada south to North Carolina and Missouri. All have edible berries.

Tiny in size and tart in flavor, these berries are usually combined with a low-acid fruit for jam or jelly. Patient, but well rewarded, is the person who picks enough for sauce or a pie.

Like cultivated species, wild gooseberries may be used green or ripe.

Gooseberry *(Ribes divaricatum)*
Picture taken on Indian Island, Washington.

12

Red-flowered Currant, Flowering Currant
Ribes sanguineum   Saxifrage Family

This member of the Gooseberry tribe is a thornless bush 2 to 10 feet high, and is best known as a flowering shrub. The upper surface of the deciduous, three- to five-lobed leaves is dark green with a lighter under surface that is matted with very fine hairs.

Early in April, and on into May, the small, bright-red flowers, in drooping clusters, create an attractive stopover for migrating humming-birds. The clusters of globe-shaped berries are blue-black, covered with a chalky bloom, ripening in July and August.

Red-flowered Currant is found growing at low elevations, along streams, in coastal forest, and along roads, from western British Columbia to northwestern California.

All the many species of Currants found growing across the United States and Canada produce edible fruit, some more palatable than others. They were an important Indian food that was soon adopted by early settlers. You may have to acquire a taste for the Red-flowered Currant, and we think cooking improves the flavor. They make good jelly, combined with Oregon Grape, which usually is found growing nearby. Try them dried to use like raisins.

Red-flowered Currant *(Ribes sanguineum)*
Picture taken on Marrowstone Island, Washington.

13

Salmon Berry
Rubus spectabilis

Rose Family

The tender young shoots of the Salmon Berry were steamed by Pacific Northwest Indians to eat with their dried salmon, and the color of the fruit resembles that of freshly baked salmon.

This deciduous shrub grows to about 6 to 8 feet tall, with stems that are usually erect. These glossy brown stems have shreddy yellow bark, and some bear weak thorns. The fuzzy leaflets are usually separated into three parts, each leaf part measuring about 3 inches long. The edges of the leaflets are saw-toothed.

The fuchsia-red flowers appear almost before the leaves, from March to June. The fruit, bright yellow to red in color, was considered by the Indians too soft to dry, but they did use this bland fruit fresh.

Salmon Berries grow in peaty soil in moist areas below 3000 feet. The range is from California to Alaska and Idaho.

Salmon Berries make a delicious jam or jelly, with a unique flavor that combines well with meats, especially beef and pork. The fruit deteriorates rapidly, so it must be used as soon as possible after picking.

Salmon Berry marmalade recipe is on page 55.

Salmon Berry *(Rubus spectabilis)*
Picture taken on Hood Canal near Hoodsport, Washington.

Thimbleberry
Rubus parviflorus

Rose Family

Thimbleberry, a common, deciduous shrub without thorns, varies in height from 2 feet in dry soil to 4 to 7 feet in damp soil. Erect stems with smooth to shreddy bark have short branches that support large, "maple-like" leaves. Large white blossoms appear in May in contrast to an almost solid-green background of leaves. By July or August these flowers have changed into bright red berries shaped more like a thin, flat cap than a thimble.

Found growing in open woods and along roads from low to mountain elevations, Thimbleberries prefer moist areas. Even in dry regions, they can be found along streams. Distribution is from southern Alaska to western Ontario and south to California and New Mexico.

Deliciously tart when eaten raw, they are soft, and separate very easily from the receptacle. This makes them easier and more fun to be "canned" fresh from the bush. A nutritional treat when added fresh to cereal, cream and honey. Try substituting Thimbleberries for Blackberries in cake (p. 51), or add to muffins and pancakes.

Thimbleberry *(Rubus parviflorus)*
Picture taken near Hoodsport, Washington.

Trailing Blackberry, Wild Blackberry, Brambleberry
Rubus ursinus   **Rose Family**

The uncrowned king of all wild berries, or at least the most sought after. Each Wild Blackberry vine may creep 20 feet or more over logs, vegetation and rocks. This thorny, shrubby vine has toothed, three- to five-part leaves growing alternately on the stems. White, five-petaled flowers appear in May or June, depending on the elevation. The male flower may be 1½ inches across, while the female, usually on a separate vine, is about half as large. Some berries are ripe by July and continue into August.

Within two years after a forest area has been either logged or burned you will usually find berries. They thrive in semishade but must have some sunshine. The Trailing Blackberry is found up to 3500 feet on the Cascade Mountains, and in coastal areas. Various species of blackberry are found throughout most of the continent of North America.

Truly a gift of love is a Blackberry pie. For those who do not already have a favorite recipe see page 56. Delicious raw, or cooked into jams, jellies, syrup, juice, or cake (p. 51).

Trailing Blackberry *(Rubus ursinus)*.
Picture taken near Hood Canal, Washington.

Black Raspberry, Blackcap
Rubus leucodermis   **Rose Family**

Unlike the Trailing Blackberry, this shrub may have upright shoots. Some stems may be trailing, but all are whitish in color and very thorny. The leaves, comprising three to five toothed leaflets, grow alternately on the stems. The underside of these leaflets is very silvery. White, five-petaled flowers blossom in small clusters in April and May. The fruit resembles the common Red Raspberry, except that it is black and bristly. Depending on the elevation, you will find it ripe in July or August.

The Black Raspberry must have lots of sunshine and coarse dry soil. Often found along roads, or in recently bulldozed areas. Common among the Olympic and Cascade Mountains. Various species of Wild Raspberry grow throughout the United States.

These are rather bland berries, but can be enjoyed raw when tossed into Jello and cream (p. 52) or cooked into jams, jellies, juices (p. 54), or syrup (p. 58). Combine with a more acid berry for improved flavor. Use Blackberry recipes for pies and cake.

Black Raspberry *(Rubus leucodermis)*
Picture taken at Potlatch, Washington.

17

Creeping Rubus
Rubus pedatus   **Rose Family**

An exquisite, tiny plant that may easily escape the novice berry picker. We first discovered it on the edge of a bank near Blue Huckleberry bushes. The thin vine, bearing occasional (three to five) lobated leaves, grows only a foot or so long. Without careful inspection, one might mistake it for Wild Strawberry, except for the fruit. White, five-petaled flowers appear from May to July, and it may bear both blooms and berries at the same time. The red berries have from one to six parts or druplets each. Look for them in July and August.

Creeping Rubus is found in the forest regions of the Olympic and Cascade Mountains in semishade.

Edible raw, these berries are rather bland. Because of their very small size and relative scarcity, these might best be left for the birds and animals.

Creeping Rubus *(Rubus pedatus)*
Picture taken in the Olympic Mountains behind Lake Cushman, Washington.

18

Himalaya Blackberry
Rubus procerus   Rose Family

Himalaya and Cut-Leaf Blackberries, two escapes from cultivation, are often confused, as they grow in the same areas and bear fruit about the same time. Look at the leaves carefully; whereas the Himalaya has three to five oval leaflets in a palmate shape, the Cut-Leaf has a really incised leaf. Himalaya leaves are toothed and grow alternately on sprawling stems, which have hooked spines. The flower has five petals that vary from white to pink. The berry is larger and seemingly seedier than that of the Trailing Blackberry. You will find Himalayas ripe in late August and September.

Softer and sweeter than the Cut-Leaf, Himalaya berries can be used in the same ways; however, they spoil more rapidly.

Himalaya Blackberry *(Rubus procerus)*
Picture taken near Quilcene, Washington.

19

Cut-Leaf Blackberry, Evergreen Blackberry
Rubus laciniatus   **Rose Family**

This species, like the Himalaya, originated in the Old World. Some pioneer planted it in the West, where it promptly escaped cultivation and grew wild. Stout vines, well armed with hooked thorns, grow up to 10 feet long and form dense thickets, climbing over anything in their path. Sharp-pointed, incised leaflets number from one to five. The color of the blossom varies from rose to pink. The large berry which follows the flower is black, firm, and ripe in late August and September.

Commonly found by roadsides and in damp areas from western Washington to northern California.

Very edible raw, delicious in pies, great for jelly, a little seedy for jam, and superb when made into syrup (p. 58) or juice. May be substituted in any Blackberry or Huckleberry recipe.

Cut-Leaf Blackberry *(Rubus laciniatus)*
Picture taken near Quilcene, Washington.

20

Wild Strawberry
Fragaria spp.   **Rose Family**

Wild Strawberries were used by the Indians for flavoring meat and making stews.

This low-growing plant may be 3 to 16 inches tall, and many species are not unlike the cultivated varieties. Its three-part leaves have saw-toothed edges. The white flowers, with five petals, appear from April to June. The fruit, red when ripe, is a miniature version of the domestic Strawberry.

Its range includes most of the states, excluding exceptionally dry areas. Its habitat extends from sea beaches to high elevations, and open areas to shady woods.

Wild Strawberries are best eaten right off the plant, because of their small size and scarcity. They may be combined with other fruit for use in any standard Strawberry recipe. Frozen or uncooked jams best preserve the subtle Strawberry flavor. Recipe on page 54.

Wild Strawberry *(Fragaria* spp.)
Picture taken near Lake Cushman, Washington.

Wild Rose
Rosa spp.   Rose Family

The Wild Rose is recognized as a familiar deciduous shrub almost everywhere in North America. It varies from a low bush to a large shrub; all are armed with thorns. The usually smooth and glossy, saw-toothed leaflets are five to seven to a leaf.

Fragrant, white-to-dark-pink, five-petaled flowers beautify the countryside from May to July. Orange-to-red seed pods (hips) are ripe in August, and in some places they are good all winter.

Wild Roses are found growing from low to high elevations, along streams and roads, and in open woods, often forming thorny thickets. There are over 100 species scattered throughout this continent.

Use the petals of the flowers for tea, salads, jelly, and for candying. Rose-hip juice is well known for being six to 24 times richer in Vitamin C than orange juice. When eaten fresh, some hips taste like fresh apples. Try them baked in breads, fresh in salads, or dried for teas. Harvesting rose hips beats buying commercially prepared Vitamin C! See recipe on page 58.

Wild Rose *(Rosa* spp.)
Picture taken on Marrowstone Island, Washington.

Indian Plum, Oso Berry, Bird Cherry, Skunk Bush, Indian Peach
Osmaronia cerasiformis   **Rose Family**

This shrub or small tree ranges from 3 to 18 feet tall, and emits a strong odor when bruised. The leaves are tapering, 3 to 5 inches long, with smooth edges. Even before the leaves are out, however, fragrant white clusters of flowers hang from the stems, heralding the beginning of spring. The bluish-black, smooth, oblong plums have a large seed and a rather bitter taste.

The range is from British Columbia to California, along coastal areas, roads, and on semiopen waste areas west of the Cascades.

We made a strong-flavored but good-tasting jelly from the fruit.

Indian Plum *(Osmaronia cerasiformis)*
Picture taken near Hood Canal School, Shelton, Washington.

Bitter Cherry
Prunus emarginata   Rose Family

In low, coastal areas, Bitter Cherry will be a good-sized tree up to 60 feet tall, with straight branches pointing upward. On dry slopes at higher elevations, look for a low, often crooked shrub. The dirty-gray-brown bark can usually be peeled off in horizontal strips and has a pungent odor when bruised. The deciduous, finely toothed leaves are oblong, tapering to tip, ½ inch to 4 inches long, having rounded bases on thin short stems.

Masses of flat clusters of fragrant white flowers may be seen during April and May. The bright red, pea-sized Cherries are ripe by July and on through August.

Bitter Cherries are found along streams and roads, and in open woods to 3000 feet, from British Columbia to southern California, and east to Montana.

Though bitter tasting, the inviting red fruit can be thirst quenching. **Remember to always discard the pit or seed.** It contains cyanide, a poison, which is destroyed by cooking. An excellent jelly can be made by following the pectin recipe for Choke or Bitter Cherry jelly (p. 55).

Bitter Cherry *(Prunus emarginata)*
Picture taken near Maytown, Washington.

24

Western Choke Cherry
Prunus demissa

Rose Family

Frequently a large shrub, the Choke Cherry can become a small tree up to 25 feet tall, with a trunk 8 inches through. The 2- to 4-inch dark-green, deciduous leaves are oval, wider above the middle, sharp-pointed, with finely saw-toothed edges.

The long, tapering clusters of white blossoms appear usually in May, after the leaves are nearly full grown. By August the ripening red-to-purple pea-sized Cherries are bending the branches.

Possibly the most widely distributed American wild fruit, Choke Cherries are found in dry places and along streams, from the Arctic Circle to Mexico, and coast to coast.

A bit puckery tasting, they are excellent thirst quenchers, and make a fine jelly (p. 55). **Warning:** discard seed when eating raw cherries.

Western Choke Cherry *(Prunus demissa)*
Picture taken along the Naches River, Washington.

Service Berry, June Berry, Shadbush, Sarvis Berry, Saskatoon Berry, Sugar Pear, Indian Pear
Amelanchier spp.

Rose Family

A native of many areas, called by several common names, this deciduous shrub is easily recognized by its alternate, roundish leaf that is saw-toothed around the upper part. From a scrubby bush 2 feet high, it varies to a large shrub or small tree 15 feet tall.

Showy clusters of white blossoms occur during April and May. Early in the summer the berries turn from red to blue-black, when they are ripe. They last until fall, depending on elevation.

Look for Service Berry growing in open woods, along streams and roads, in swamps, even on rocky slopes, from Alaska to Newfoundland, and south to California and the Gulf of Mexico.

All the some 25 species are edible, having a pleasant, sweet flavor, and may be eaten raw, cooked, or dried. Western Indians often used the dried berries for pemmican or, after drying, pounded into large loaves. Fresh berries are delicious in pancakes, muffins, pies, jams or jellies. They resemble Blueberries in appearance, texture and taste, so you may substitute Service Berries in any Blueberry recipe.

Service Berry *(Amelanchier* spp.)
Picture taken at Quilcene, Washington.

26

Black Hawthorn, Thorn Plum, Thorn Apple, Black Haw, Blackthorn

Crataegus spp.   **Rose Family**

The deciduous Hawthorns range from a shrub to a bushy tree up to 20 feet tall. Sharp thorns ½ to 1½ inches long are prominent on all species. Their leaves, on short stems, are oval in shape, ranging from toothed to lobed. The smaller branches make a weak zig-zag. Fragrant five-petaled flowers blossom in April and May. The fruit appears in July or August in the form of purplish-black miniature apples.

The Hawthorns may be found coast-to-coast near streams in woods and thickets. Common in the West.

The apples may be eaten fresh but do contain five large seeds. The fruit is high in sugar but low in fats and proteins, and withers quickly. Indians did dry them for pemmican and they can be used in jams, jellies or muffins.

Black Hawthorn *(Crataegus* spp.)
Picture taken in Tenino, Washington.

27

Pacific Crab Apple, Oregon Crab Apple
Malus fusca   **Rose Family**

Pacific Crab Apple is often shrub-like, growing in thickets, or is a small tree 30 feet high, its branches covered with thorn-like spurs. The deciduous leaves, growing alternately, are oval, tapering to a point at the tip, some irregularly lobed, with sharply toothed edges.

Blooming in April and May, the fragrant, white or pinkish flat-topped flower clusters look like small typical apple blossoms. Clusters of oblong-oval, half-inch apples, yellow, tinged with red, start to ripen in August and September.

Crab Apples like to grow in moist open woods and along the coast, from the Aleutian Islands, along the coastal regions of Alaska and British Columbia, west of the Cascade Mountains of Washington and Oregon, to a southern limit in Sonoma and Plumas counties, California.

These tart little apples were used by the early settlers for jelly, preserves, pickles, and for sauces and pies. We make a tart jelly without pectin that is good with meat or fowl.

A few really ripe wild Crab Apples are good to snack on raw; however, it's probably best to avoid eating very many this way. All apple seeds contain cyanide, a poison which cooking renders harmless.

Pacific Crab Apple *(Malus fusca)*
Picture taken near Maytown, Washington.

28

Mountain Ash
Sorbus spp.

Rose Family

There are at least two (disputed) species of Mountain Ash in the Pacific states, very much alike, which may reach a height of 17 feet, with long thin stems. The bark appears to be grayish brown and spotted. Its leaves are compound, with from nine to 13 leaflets on a stem. The flowers are a waxy white, with 30 to 60 flowers in a cluster. When the fruit appears, it is globe shaped and a glossy scarlet.

Mountain Ash grows above the 3000-foot level in the coastal ranges and above 4000 feet in the mountains in the interior of Washington and Oregon. Mountain Ash prefers semiopen areas with well drained soil.

When eaten raw, the berries are very bitter and mealy. Wait until the area has had a good frost before picking. Best used for jelly and jam. They are low in fat and protein, but high in carbohydrates, with quite an amount of tannin. The Indians ate the berries fresh, and also dried and ground into meal.

Since the berries remain on the stems throughout the winter, they provide food for many animals and birds, as well as man.

Mountain Ash *(Sorbus* spp.)
Picture taken at Mosquito Meadows, near Mt. Adams, Washington.

29

Crowberry, Heathberry
Empetrum nigrum   **Crowberry Family**

Incredible as it may seem, we first spotted this elusive plant from our car window while traveling 50 miles per hour. A low-growing, 2- to 6-inch, freely branching evergreen shrub, the Crowberry resembles Heather. Tiny, glossy, needle-like leaves, 1/8 to ½ inch long, grow alternately or whorled. During June and July, Crowberry has a very small purple bloom. We found the blue-black, round berries still ripe in late September.

Crowberry grows in moist, rocky, open, coastal areas, and in peat bogs. The distribution is circumpolar, from Alaska to Greenland to Siberia, south to northwestern California, and east to the Atlantic; also in Europe, and in Chile. It grows sparingly along the coastline in the Pacific states, and on Mount Rainier, Washington.

Crowberry is reported to be a vital survival food for the Eskimo. It is edible raw or cooked.

Crowberry *(Empetrum nigrum)*
Picture taken about 6 miles south of Gold Beach, Oregon.

Sumac, Smooth Sumac, Scarlet Sumac
Rhus glabra   **Sumac Family**

Although it is classed as a shrub, Sumac may range from 3 to 20 feet in height. Slender, pointed leaflets, 11 to 31 in number, constitute a leaf that is a foot or more long. The branches are stout and the bark is smooth. In May, tiny, greenish-yellow flowers bloom in a compact cone. Velvety, red fruit ripens by September or October, and stays on the branches throughout the winter. Since rain leaches the fruit, collect the clusters in October.

Common in the United States, Sumac is found east of the Cascade Mountains in Washington. West of the Cascades, wild Sumac is popular as a garden shrub.

To prepare a cool, refreshing drink similar to lemonade, break up the clusters and over the fruit pour boiling water. Steep 30-40 minutes. Strain carefully to remove all the fuzz, add honey to taste, and cool. This drink may be enjoyed hot or cold. Add a sprig of mint for added flavor.

Note: **Poison Sumac** does **not** grow in Washington but is an eastern species; its fruit is white or creamy yellow.

Sumac *(Rhus glabra)*
Picture taken near Union, Washington.

California Wild Grape
Vitis californica

Grape Family

Wild Grapes look almost exactly like their cultivated relatives. They have stout vines with shreddy bark, and often climb trees to 30 feet or more. Their variable, broad leaves can be three-lobed or not. May to June is the blooming period for the fragrant, greenish-yellow flowers. The smooth, purple grapes hanging in typical clusters are ripe in September and October.

We found Wild Grapes in great quantity along stream banks just by the road in the foothills of the coast ranges in California. This species is found in foothills of southwestern Oregon and most of California.

Very sweet and delicious raw, Wild Grapes can be used for jelly, jam, wine, and in any way cultivated grapes are used. For jelly we used the commercial pectin recipe for Concord Grapes (p. 53).

California Wild Grape *(Vitis californica)*
The picture was taken from the highway in Trinity National Forest, California.

32

Buffalo-berry, Soapolallie, Soap Berry, Russet Buffalo-berry

Shepherdia canadensis   Oleaster Family

The distinctive Buffalo-berry shrub may vary in height from 3 to 10 feet, or more. Oval leaves with slightly rolled edges grow alternately on rusty-spotted branches. The upper side of the leaf is dark green and smooth, in contrast to the silver, speckled with rust-brown spots, of the under side. Tiny, yellow-green clusters of unique flowers bloom around April, usually with male and female blossoms on separate shrubs. Small clusters of red-orange berries replace the blossoms by late May or June.

Preferring a well drained soil, the Buffalo-berry may be found growing with evergreens, Salal, and Arrowwood. The range is from Alaska to California and the Rockies, and east to Newfoundland.

Buffalo-berries have a high content of saponin, which produces a soapy foam when rubbed. The berries are too bitter to eat raw, but may be dried and sugared to be used like currants. The Indians used them for pudding, or whipped the berries into a froth to be served as a topping or dessert. These berries are very juicy, so may be used in a tart jelly.

Buffalo-berry *(Shepherdia canadensis)*
Picture taken on Marrowstone Island, Washington.

33

Mountain Dogwood
Cornus Nuttallii   **Dogwood Family**

"The Legend of the Dogwood" and the part this bushy shrub plays in the Easter story are well known. Its size ranges from a 10-foot shrub to a symmetrical tree 80 feet tall. In the spring it has glossy, dark leaves with veins that curve almost parallel to the outside edges. By fall they usually turn reddish in color. From April to June, and sometimes again in September, showy white blossoms decorate the woods. Appearing before the leaves, four to seven large white "petals" (bracts) surround a central mound of tiny green florets. This mound develops into a cluster of small red berries in the fall.

This species of Dogwood prefers north slopes of mountains in open woods, from British Columbia to southern California and east to Idaho. Smaller species also occur within the range, especially along streams.

The early settlers ate the berries raw and cooked. We found them very bitter in flavor raw, but because they contain enough protein, carbohydrate and fat to sustain life, they are a valuable survival food.

Mountain Dogwood *(Cornus Nuttallii)*
Picture taken near Lilliwaup, Washington.

34

Bunchberry, Dwarf Cornel, Pigeon Berry
Cornus canadensis   Dogwood Family

Forming decorative carpets, this low-growing, nonwoody herb is really a relative of the tall, woody tree, the Mountain Dogwood. The leaves grow in two or three opposite pairs in a whorl at the top of the short stem. Deciduous, oval, and tapering to a point at the tip and base, the individual leaves are very similar to those of other Dogwoods, with almost parallel veining. Blooming in April and May, and sometimes again in August and September, the typical Dogwood blossom has four white bracts surrounding the greenish center mound of tiny flowers. By August and September the flowers are replaced by a mound of small, bright red berries.

Bunchberry prefers to grow over rotten logs and around old stumps in moist forests. Distribution is from Alaska to northern California and east to the Atlantic coast.

We found these bland little berries incredibly edible, delicious when combined with Red Huckleberries, Blue Huckleberries, Blackberries or Bitter Cherries. All are usually ripe at the same time.

A source of quick energy for hikers, Pigeon Berries are also choice bird food, as one of the common names implies.

Bunchberry *(Cornus canadensis)*
Picture taken at about 1500 feet, near Lake Cushman, Washington.

35

Madrone, Madroño, Madrona, Arbutus
Arbutus Menziesii   **Heath Family**

The exfoliation of reddish-brown bark, leaving a smooth surface of green, brown or red is characteristic of the Madrone. A heavy, branched tree, it grows 10 to 100 feet tall, with a widely spreading crown. The alternate, thick, glossy, evergreen leaves are oval to oblong, 3 to 5 inches long. Clusters of creamy-white bell-shaped blossoms appear in May. The round orange-red berries that ripen in late summer and on into fall are a great source of food for migrating birds. A noticeable tree any time of the year, the Madrone is especially beautiful with its colorful, loose clusters of fruit hanging heavily from the branches.

Madrone grows in rocky soil on wooded slopes, from British Columbia southward to lower California.

Edible raw or dried, the rather bitter tasting berries are better cooked into a sauce, adding honey or sugar to taste.

Madrone *(Arbutus Menziesii)*
Picture taken near Brinnon, Washington.

Manzanita
Arctostaphylos spp.

Heath Family

A shrub up to 8 feet high, erect or spreading, most with fuzzy twigs. Reddish bark peels off the branches in thin curls. The winter-persistent leaves are oval and pointed. Flowers are creamy, pinkish white to yellowish brown. The fruit is red or brown, slightly fuzzy, and mealy. The range is from Vancouver Island and the Cascade Mountains south to Mexico, and east to Colorado. The northern habitat is open pine woods at moderate altitudes up to about 7000 feet.

Manzanita berries are best described as survival food; however, the Indians sometimes used them in their pemmican. They can be used for making jelly or cider. For cider, crush the berries and scald with water equal in amount to the bulk of the berries. The Spanish name, Manzanita, means "little apple".

Manzanita *(Arctostaphylos* spp.)
Picture taken near Littlerock, Washington.

Kinnikinnick, Bearberry, Sandberry

Arctostaphylos Uva-ursi   **Heath Family**

Kinnikinnick grows in long runners close to the ground in open areas such as the banks along roadways. An evergreen with dark red bark, it has oblong, leathery leaves growing alternately on the stem. The pink, bell-shaped flowers are replaced by small, bright red berries in August, which continue on the vines until late fall.

Kinnikinnick prefers dry, well drained soil in pine woods, from coastal dunes to 10,000 feet. Its range is circumpolar in northern latitudes.

The Indians called the leaves, *"k'nick"*, which they used for smoking. The berries are consumed raw by animals and humans alike, but cooking will bring out their natural sweetness. Use any apple recipe to make jelly.

Kinnikinnick *(Arctostaphylos Uva-ursi)*
Picture taken near Littlerock, Washington.

38

Salal
Gaultheria shallon   **Heath Family**

This shrub, varying from 1 to 10 feet tall, forms dense thickets in coniferous woods. Sold commercially by brush pickers to florists. The oval leaves, very leathery and thick, grow alternately on sturdy stems.

The pinkish, bell-shaped flowers hang near the ends of the stems from May to July. The round, dark blue, hairy berries appear in August, and stay on the shrub until October.

Salal grows from the coastal woods to approximately 2500 feet elevation, and ranges from British Columbia to California.

Salal berries are used for jelly, syrup, survival food, and (dried) to add to muffins or pancakes. Many people combine Oregon Grape berries with Salal for jelly, but Salal has a very fine flavor when used alone.

Salal *(Gaultheria shallon)*
Picture taken along Hood Canal, Washington.

Western Teaberry, Bush Wintergreen, Oregon Wintergreen
Gaultheria ovatifolia   Heath Family

Tea made from Teaberry leaves was used by both Indian and pioneer to reduce fever.

A short, spreading shrub, Teaberry will not grow any higher than 1 foot. The stems are reddish in color, kinky, and rather hairy. Shiny green, heart-shaped, pointed leaves alternate along trailing, hairy stems. Tiny, bell-shaped, white flowers appear among the leaves in May. These blossoms are replaced by bright red berries which are hairy and grooved into segments and hang under the stems through August and into September.

Grows in the Olympics and Cascades from 1500 feet up to 6000 feet, usually in semiopen forests of pine and Douglas Fir. Ranges from British Columbia to Idaho and California.

The berries can be eaten raw, used as a flavoring, or made into jelly, using an apple recipe.

Western Teaberry *(Gaultheria ovatifolia)*
We found them by the roadside in the Mt. Adams area, and this picture was taken above Lake Cushman, Washington, in the Olympic Mountains.

Cranberry, Pacific Cranberry, Cow Berry
Vaccinium Oxycoccus var. *intermedium*   Heath Family

When you locate Labrador Tea, you will usually find Cranberries hiding underneath. Stretching along the ground for 3 to 4 feet, this long, thin vine has small evergreen leaves growing alternately along the stem. Dainty pink flowers bloom in early summer, but the fruit does not ripen until late September or October. Round, white-to-red berries grow on thin, thread-like stems.

Cranberries prefer peaty bogs that contain sphagnum moss. Their range is from Alaska to northern California on the west coast, and Newfoundland to Virginia on the east coast.

Although the berries are smaller than the domestic variety, they have a more delightful, wild, tangy flavor. Eat them raw as in a relish (p. 57), cooked in a sauce, or in a meat recipe (p. 57).

Cranberry *(Vaccinium Oxycoccus* var. *intermedium)*
Picture taken in a sphagnum bog near Hoodsport, Washington.

Evergreen Huckleberry, Shot Huckleberry

Vaccinium ovatum, Vaccinium ovatum var. *saparosum*   Heath Family

This member of the Huckleberry tribe is a bushy evergreen shrub, growing up to 8 feet high. The small, (less than 1 inch), glossy leaves are oval to oblong, with pointed tips and finely toothed edges. Small, pink, urn-shaped flowers can be seen from March until June. It is October before the roundish, shiny-black or frosty-blue berries are ripe.

Evergreen Huckleberries are found only in moist coastal areas, from British Columbia to central California.

The ripe berries are juicy, and good raw, if a bit seedy. They are highly desirable for sauce, fresh or canned, as jelly, jam or syrups, in muffins, in pies, and in any of your favorite desserts. See Blueberry recipes.

Important wild plants economically, the Huckleberries are commercially canned, and the evergreen branches are picked for the floral industry.

Evergreen Huckleberry   Evergreen Huckleberry
(Vaccinium ovatum var. *saparosum)*   *(Vaccinium ovatum)*
Pictures taken near Hoodsport, Washington.

42

Blueberry, Blue Huckleberry, Whortleberry, Bilberry

Vaccinium spp.   **Heath Family**

Even the botanists differ when describing and classifying the numerous species of this genus. Plants range from a 1- to 8-inch shrub to a bush 6 feet high. The usually deciduous oval-to-oblong leaves, are ¼ to 1½ inches in length, with or without finely toothed edges.

Blueberries and Huckleberries have a white-to-pink bell-shaped blossom, appearing from May to July. From July to October you can find ripe berries. Some may be blue with a lighter blue bloom, and others a glossy black, all growing in the same area. Blueberries, some say, have many fine chewable seeds; Huckleberries have fewer and larger seeds. Both are delicious.

Some 35 different species of *Vaccinium* can be found in bogs, open woods and mountain meadows throughout Alaska, Canada, and the United States.

All are edible raw; however, some kinds can be improved by cooking. Use them in any of your favorite recipes and try some of ours (pp. 50, 51, 52, 56, 58).

Bilberry   Blue Huckleberry
(Vaccinium ovalifolium)   *(Vaccinium membranaceum)*

The Bilberry picture was taken on Mosquito Meadows, Mt. Adams, Washington. The Huckleberry picture was taken at 1500 feet elevation near Lake Cushman, Washington.

Red Huckleberry
Vaccinium parvifolium   **Heath Family**

The small, bright-green leaves grow alternately on the branches of a shrub 2 to 15 feet in height. The more lush the leafage on the shrub, the fewer berries you will find. In the spring, small, pink, bell-shaped flowers hang under the branches. The round, bright-red berries stay on the branches through the fall and into the winter.

Red Huckleberries inhabit cool, usually shady areas, and often grow out of old stumps, at sites of old burns, and along roadways. Commonly found in coastal forest from sea level to 1500 feet.

Red Huckleberries make delicious juicy pies (p. 56), beautifully colored jelly, using a currant recipe, and a delicious relish for meats (p. 57).

Red Huckleberry *(Vaccinium parvifolium)*
Picture taken near Lilliwaup, Washington.

Blue Elderberry, Blue-Berry Elder
Sambucus caerulea   Honeysuckle Family

Known by some Indians as "The Tree of Music" this woody, pithy-centered, erect shrub usually grows in clumps of small, round stems 6 to 20 feet high. The large, deciduous leaves comprise five to nine leaflets that grow opposite. The edges of the leaflets are finely saw-toothed.

Blue Elderberry blooms during the summer until September, displaying distinctive, flat-topped, creamy-white flower clusters 3 to 8 inches across. These large blossom "heads" are replaced by clusters of tiny, round, blue-black berries covered with white bloom when ripe in September and late fall.

You'll find Blue Elderberry in open woods, along roads, and in coniferous forest, from British Columbia to California, Alberta to Arizona and New Mexico.

Since these berries can be found in quantity, they have long been famous for wine. We like them to nibble on raw, in pancakes, waffles, muffins, jelly and pie. For a change of menu, try the blossoms dipped in batter and deep-fat fried.

Blue Elderberry *(Sambucus caerulea)*
Picture taken near Skokomish Valley, Washington.

45

Orange Honeysuckle
Lonicera ciliosa   **Honeysuckle Family**

Orange Honeysuckle climbs up shrubs and trees by spiraling around their branches. Its oval leaves appear very early in the spring, a little before the Indian Plum's. The leaves grow opposite on the stems, and have a white bloom on the under side. The end leaves join to make one disk, through which the stem grows. From the ends of these stems blossom beautiful orange, tube-shaped flowers. Several months elapse between blossoms and bunches of ripe, orange berries.

Another species, *Lonicera hispidula*, inhabits open areas in soil with good drainage; but the Orange Honeysuckle prefers the wet, shady regions below 2000 feet west of the Cascade Mountains, and shady areas at higher elevations east of the Cascades.

The berries are edible but bland. They may be used as survival food, made into a syrup (p. 58), or combined with a more acid berry for use in jelly.

Orange Honeysuckle *(Lonicera ciliosa)*
Picture taken by Hamma Hamma River in Olympic Mountains, Washington.

Black Twinberry, Bearberry Honeysuckle
Lonicera involucrata   Honeysuckle Family

Not very well known, Black Twinberry is none-the-less abundant. The shrub may stand 2 to 10 feet high, with straw-colored twigs that appear square and coarse. These stems may have fine hairs or be hairless. The oval leaves, 2 to 4 inches long, are shiny, light green, growing opposite on the branches. From the axil of the leaf, on an approximately 2-inch stem, grow two separate yellow flowers by May or June. The blossoms are replaced by a pair of shiny, black, oblong berries on a red "ruff" in July and August. These pairs suggest its name, Twinberry.

Black Twinberry grows along the cliffs above the ocean, and in wet areas from sea level to mountain slopes. Its range is east and west of the Cascade Mountains from British Columbia to northern California.

This sweet berry can be eaten raw, made into syrup (p. 58) or made into jelly. Combine with a more acid berry to improve the flavor of the jelly.

Black Twinberry *(Lonicera involucrata)*
Picture taken near Chimacum, Washington.

High-Bush Cranberry
Viburnum spp.   **Honeysuckle Family**

Not a Cranberry at all, this erect shrub has three-lobed, maple-like, opposite leaves. Deciduous and rather crinkled, the leaves turn a brilliant red in the fall. Blooming from May to June, the white or pink flowers are in showy, compact clusters of tiny florets. Clusters of bright red berries ripen in August, and in some areas they hang on the bushes until after the leaves have fallen.

High-Bush Cranberry is found in mountain woods from Alaska to Washington, south in the Cascade Mountains to central Oregon, and east to Colorado, Pennsylvania, and Newfoundland. We discovered one in someone's yard at Olympia, Washington, that was a transplant from Minnesota.

Juicy, and sweetish-sour in flavor when eaten raw, the fruit makes a uniquely flavored jelly and wine. Makes a good syrup (p. 58) for pancakes and waffles.

High-Bush Cranberry *(Viburnum* spp.)
Picture taken at Olympia, Washington.

48

Recipes

BEVERAGES

Oregon-Grape/Apple Juice

Into a six-quart saucepan put 3 cups of mashed berries, 6 medium-sized apples cut into quarters, and 2 cups water. Cook about 10 minutes. Add water if needed. Remove from heat, and put through strainer. Return the juice to the pan, together with ½ to 1 cup sugar, depending on the tartness of the apples. Stir and cook until sugar dissolves. Remove from heat and pour into jars or bottles. The juice tastes similar to the commercial cranberry-apple juice. The recipe may be doubled. If the apples are very firm, slice into smaller pieces and cook a little longer.

Thick Berry Shake

You may have to eat this with a spoon. Add more milk if you like a thinner consistency.

1 cup milk

1 cup ice cream or ice milk

1 cup wild berries of your choice

1/3 cup sugar (may vary with tartness of the berries)

Combine all ingredients in the electric blender. Beat until smooth and fluffy.

Tea

Tea may be made from the crushed leaves of most berries. Dry them thoroughly in the sun, or in a very low-temperature oven with the door slightly open. Blue Huckleberry leaves have more flavor than the leaves of Red Huckleberry, Blackberry or Strawberry. Most berry leaves contain medicinal value but little flavor. Either combine with regular tea or add a leaf or two of wild mint. Be sure to collect leaves in areas not contaminated by drifting poisonous sprays.

CAKE AND MUFFINS

Trailing Blackberry Cake

½ cup butter or margarine

1½ cups sugar

1 egg

1 cup buttermilk

1 tsp soda

2 cups sifted flour

1 cup berries (fresh, frozen, or drained canned)

½ tsp cinnamon

Cream butter and sugar. Add beaten egg, mixing well. Add sifted flour, spice and soda alternately with milk. Fold in berries with last portion of flour. Pour batter into greased and floured pan, 9 inches by 12 inches. Bake 40 minutes at 350°, or until done. Any of the blackberries, huckleberries, blueberries, service berries or cranberries may be substituted for Trailing Blackberries. Serve warm with whipped cream or topping, or frost with your favorite icing.

Huckleberry or Blueberry Muffins

1 cup blueberries or huckleberries

1 cup milk

¼ cup oil

1/3 cup sugar

2 cups flour

½ tsp salt

3 tsp baking powder

1 egg

Beat egg, add milk and oil, and gradually add to sifted dry ingredients. Stir only until flour is dampened. Gently fold in berries last.

Bacon may be added with the berries for variation. Cut ½ lb bacon into small pieces, and brown. Drain off the grease and use ¼ cup of it in place of oil in the recipe. Add bacon bits with the berries.

51

CANDY AND DESSERTS

Fruit Leather

Purée raw or cooked fruit, sweeten to taste with honey or sugar. (If using berries with large seeds, rub purée through a sieve.)

Cover cookie sheet with plastic film, taping corners; pour fruit on sheet to desired thickness, spreading evenly. Place in a dehydrator or an oven set at lowest possible temperature for about 24 hours or until it feels dry. Brace the oven door open an inch during drying. Cut into sections and roll up. Store in freezer—it takes about 10 minutes to thaw enough to eat.

When using fruits such as peaches, pears, apricots and apples, add ascorbic acid to the purée to prevent color loss.

Black-Raspberry or Blackcap Dessert

For a quick treat, we like to use fresh Blackcaps tossed with fruit gelatin and cream. Use any berry-flavored gelatin (raspberry is our choice) and prepare according to directions on the package. Before it has completely set, fold in a cup of whipped cream or topping and 2 cups berries. Place in refrigerator until set.

For the large-size package of gelatin, double the amount of cream and berries.

Fresh Berry Meringues

Use 1½ to 2 cups wild berries, 1 tsp lemon juice, ¼ to ½ cup orange juice, ¾ cup powdered sugar, and a half pint of whipping cream.

Whip the cream. Combine other ingredients in blender until puréed. Fold into whipped cream and place in shallow pan. Freeze until firm.

Meanwhile, prepare your meringue shells. Scoop the fruit mixture into individual shells about 10 minutes before serving. You may top this with a fresh, sweetened serving of fruit.

JAMS AND JELLIES

Wild Grape Jelly

    5 cups juice

    1 box powdered pectin

    7 cups sugar

    Wash and crush about 8 cups ripe wild grapes. Add 1½ cups water and cover; simmer for 10 minutes. Place in jelly bag; squeeze to extract juice.

    Place juice and pectin in a six- to eight-quart saucepan. Bring to hard boil for 1 minute, stirring occasionally. Add sugar; bring to full rolling boil (a boil that cannot be stirred down), stirring constantly. Boil hard for 1 minute. Remove from heat, skim if necessary. Pour at once into hot, sterilized jars; seal with 1/8 inch paraffin, or use jars that seal with two-part metal lids.

Oregon-Grape Jelly

    4 cups juice

    1 box powdered pectin

    5½ cups sugar

    Proceed same as for making Wild Grape Jelly.

Fairybell Jelly

    3 cups juice

    3 cups sugar

    juice of 1 lemon

    Follow Choke Cherry Jelly Recipe on page 55 for extracting juice. Place juice and sugar in six-quart saucepan. Bring to a rolling boil, stirring constantly. Boil several minutes until mixture reaches jelly stage. Jelly stage is reached when the mixture sheets from the spoon.

JAMS AND JELLIES

Wild Strawberry Jam — Uncooked method

1. Measure 2 cups wild strawberries and 1/8 cup lemon juice into a two-quart kettle; mix well. Sift in, slowly, ½ package powdered pectin. Stir well. Set aside for 25 minutes, stirring occasionally.

2. Add ½ cup light corn syrup. Mix well.

3. Gradually stir 2½ cups sugar into crushed fruit. Warm to 100° F. No hotter.

4. Store in jelly glasses or freezer containers with lids. Store in freezer (or may be kept in refrigerator for 2 or 3 weeks).

Above recipe may be doubled and used for all species of black-berries, blueberries, huckleberries, black raspberries and service berries. If berries are quite tart, omit the lemon juice.

Purée

The easiest way to make purée for candy, jam, fruit soup or dessert is to put raw berries, either fresh or frozen, into a blender; then, if the seeds are large, rub through a sieve. Purée is made without a blender by mashing ripe fruit before pressing through a sieve. With some firm fruit such as apples, cherries and rose hips, cook the fruit slightly with a very small amount of water. If possible, avoid cooking most berries, to hold fresh flavor and save precious vitamins.

JAMS AND JELLIES

Choke Cherry or Bitter Cherry Jelly

3½ cups juice

1 package powdered pectin

juice of 1 lemon

4½ cups sugar

Wash about 8 cups cherries. Place in saucepan with about ½ cup water. Simmer, covered, 10 minutes. Place cooked fruit in jelly bag, letting juice drip through bag.

Place strained juice, lemon juice and pectin in a six- to eight-quart saucepan. Bring to a hard boil; boil 1 minute, stirring occasionally. Add sugar. Bring to full rolling boil (a boil that cannot be stirred down). Boil hard for 1 minute, stirring constantly. Remove from heat, skim if necessary. Pour at once into hot, sterilized glasses, and seal with 1/8 inch melted paraffin, or use jars that seal with two-piece metal lids. This recipe may also be used for High-Bush Cranberries.

Use the same recipe for Indian Plum, except decrease sugar by ½ cup and add ¼ cup lemon juice.

Salmon-Berry/Orange Jelly or Marmalade

Carefully examine inside caps of ripe berries, and wash. To about 6 cups berries, add 1 cup water. Boil gently for 5 minutes. Mash berries and put through sieve. Discard seeds. To sieved pulp add the juice of one orange. For every cup combined juice add one cup sugar and mix in six-quart pan. Stir and boil until mixture reaches the jelly stage. Remove from heat. Pour into glasses and seal.

PIES

Baked Blackberry Pie (Huckleberry or Blueberry Pie)

Place crust in 9-inch pie plate. To 5 cups berries add 1¼ cups sugar mixed with 3 tbs tapioca and pinch of salt. Stir lightly. Spread berries in unbaked crust. Put a pat of butter on top of berries before adding top crust. Bake pie at 425° for 15 minutes. Turn down heat to 375° and continue to bake another 30 or 40 minutes. Serve warm or cooled.

For Red Huckleberries, add 2 more tbs tapioca or cornstarch. Blueberries need some cinnamon for flavor. The amount of sugar depends on the tartness of your fruit.

Himalaya or Cut-Leaf Blackberries will cook down more than the Trailing Blackberry, so use a cup more berries and 1 tbs more thickening.

Unbaked Blackberry Pie

4 cups blackberries

¾ cup sugar

1 cup water (or juice drained from frozen berries)

1/3 cup cornstarch

2 tbs lemon juice

Crush 1 cup berries, blend sugar, cornstarch and water, and add to berries. Cook over medium heat, stirring constantly until mixture thickens. Remove from heat. Stir in remaining berries and lemon juice. Pour into baked pie shell. Top with whipped cream or other prepared toppings.

You can use Blueberries, but decrease the sugar to ½ cup.

RELISHES AND MEAT SAUCES

Wild Cranberry Relish

Wash and pick-over 4 cups cranberries. Put through food grinder. Squeeze the juice from two oranges and save to put in relish. Cut up oranges and put through grinder, discarding only the seeds. Combine cranberries, oranges and juice with 2 cups sugar. Let stand at room temperature for an hour or so. Mix ingredients thoroughly again, and store in covered dish in refrigerator. Delicious served with turkey, chicken, or ham.

Red Huckleberry Sauce

This makes a good substitute for cranberry sauce to serve on turkey, chicken, ham, or pork. We freeze our berries on large, flat pans, and later transfer them to covered containers. This way, the berries are loose and easy to use, right from the freezer without bothering to thaw.

For this recipe, measure out 2 cups frozen berries and place in medium-size saucepan with just enough water to cover the bottom of the pan. Bring to a boil, stirring occasionally. Add 1 cup sugar and bring to a second boil. Turn down the heat to simmer, and cook for 3 or 4 minutes. Remove from the burner and cool.

Red Huckleberry Glaze

One cup Red Huckleberries combined with ½ cup brown sugar and 1 tbs lemon juice makes a delicious glaze for meat loaf. Boil ingredients until the sugar dissolves, and pour half over meat loaf before baking. Pour the remainder over the meat about half-way through baking time. You may want to make extra sauce to use when serving.

The pioneers and Indians used fruit with their meat, probably to mask the wild flavor and to add moisture to dry meat.

Red Huckleberries are plentiful, easy to pick, and remain on the bush for a long time without spoiling.

SYRUPS

Huckleberry Syrup

2 cups huckleberry juice

2 cups sugar

2 cups white corn syrup (clear)

Extract juice as for jelly, or use 2 cups whole, cooked, unsweetened berries. Heat juice to boiling, add sugar, stir until dissolved. Add corn syrup, heat to boiling, and simmer about 5 minutes. Seal in hot sterilized jars. Delicious on ice cream, pancakes, or waffles. Almost any wild fruit may be substituted for huckleberries.

Rose Hip Purée

Remove the stems and blossom ends of the rose hips, and wash in cold water. Put hips in a pan with enough water to cover. Bring to a boil and simmer until soft, about 10 to 15 minutes. Do not overcook. Put entire mass through a blender, or rub through a sieve. Store in freezer. The purée may be used in many ways; for instance, it's delicious sweetened with honey for a spread on muffins or toast, as a sauce when sweetened to taste with honey, or made into fruit leather (page 52).

NOTE: Rose Hips should not be cooked in an aluminum or copper pan, for the metal could destroy the Vitamin C. Always use stainless steel, glass or earthenware pans.

Rose Hip Syrup

Prepare rose hips as for purée (above), adding slightly more water. To this thinner purée add one part honey to two parts rose hip purée.

Honey

For health's sake, use honey instead of sugar when possible. The only problem is that honey will mask subtle fruit flavors. Do not substitute more than ½ the sugar with honey in jams or jellies. Don't use with strawberries or bland berries. Be sure to use a larger kettle than usual when cooking with honey, as it tends to foam.

GLOSSARY

Alternate: Growing in any arrangement along a stem that is neither opposite nor whorled.

Bract: A specialized leaf or leaf-like part, usually situated at the base of a flower or flower head.

Bloom: A whitish powdery deposit or coating on the surface of certain fruits, such as Blue Elderberry.

Compound Leaf: A leaf composed of two or more separate blades or leaflets on a common leaf stalk or support.

Circumpolar: Occurring around the pole, as of arctic plants found in Alaska, Canada, Scandinavia and Siberia.

Deciduous: Falling, as the leaves of nonevergreen trees.

Dentate: Leaves whose edges are toothed and the teeth point outward.

Floret: A small flower; one of the closely clustered small flowers that make up a flower head.

Leaflet: One of the divisions or blades of a compound leaf.

Lobed: Having divisions extending less than halfway to the middle of the base.

Opposite: Growing directly across from each other on the stem.

Palmate: Shaped like an open palm with fingers extended.

Pemmican: Dried meat pounded into a paste with melted fat and dried fruits, pressed into cakes.

Receptacle: Expanded portion of the stem that bears the organs of a single flower, or the florets of a flower head.

Species: An interfertile group of organisms bearing common characters which distinguish them from other groups.

Veins: A system of ducts forming the principal framework of a leaf.

Whorled: Arranged in circular array around a single node or joint on the stem.

INDEX

INDEX

INDEX

NOTES

NOTES